Tahrir Suite

Tahrir Suite

Poems

Matthew Shenoda

TRIQUARTERLY BOOKS/NORTHWESTERN UNIVERSITY PRESS

EVANSTON, ILLINOIS

TriQuarterly Books
Northwestern University Press
www.nupress.northwestern.edu

Printed in the United States of America

10 9 8 7 6 5 4 3 2 1

Library of Congress Cataloging-in-Publication Data

Shenoda, Matthew, author.
    Tahrir suite : poems / Matthew Shenoda.
      pages cm
    Includes bibliographical references.
    ISBN 978–0-8101–3024–1 (pbk. : alk. paper)—ISBN 978-0-8101-6815-2 (ebook)
    1. Egypt—Poetry. I. Title.
    PS3619.H4538T34 2014
    811.6—dc23

2014004814

For Christina, my unabridged spirit.

For Dimyana, the bearer of our name, antecedent, and song.

For Mama, Abuna Pimen, Maryann, Makarios, and Seraphim.

For Pops and Minreet, always.

&

For all the people of Egypt.

I don't live anywhere. Not anymore. I'm redefining home. *Home* is related to *certainty*.

—BENJAMIN ALIRE SÁENZ

The truth is an offense, but not a sin.

—BOB MARLEY

CONTENTS

Tahrir Suite

In the country of waiting
Time is the essence that threads
Modernity to antiquity

I

The Eruption

Shortly after sunrise Tekla descended
A ladder made of fallen palms
Down from the roof of his sleep
He entered the courtyard aside a mud wall
Eyes half shut to the saline air
He meditated on the sleek dust that cooled his feet
Gazed east at the sun coming over Lake Arun

Isis could not make out the shadows
Probed by her own remembrance
She made solace from the warmth of her blanket
Knew this day could not be like any other
They would reach the city in short order
Partake of the migration that was to come

They would greet their crossing
But first an eruption

All who gather know, you have to feel it to reveal it
Sudden in your own infancy
You realize the ground is something new

The protesters converging in a single place
Made a home of something old
Began the chants that transform night

If order can preserve us
We'll indicate desire in every motion
Walk the same route on every morning
Hum the same song on every evening

The skies of this earth, a remnant
Foretold before its own story
Amorphous like squalor in the night
We are made to understand the cavernous heart

Isis searched and searched for reciprocity
Dreamed it'd been attained before
Committed to her memory
Assured it was hers to find

Darkness an outlet
Light a small shadow
When a walk of ire becomes what is known
A mask fractured by cold independence
Boldness is the sole remedy

This new language, strangely palatal
Every word a rendition
Unmistaken like the scent of sea
Permeating her skin

This is a crucial thing
That one cannot live without the threads of dignity
That one cannot live without acceptance
That one cannot live without a sun to guide

Ekphrasis was her name
She was the child of an open song
That carried its melody from disparate shores
And buried its rhythm in the hot-touch sand

The skylark trills into morning light
And they know this sound can bring them back
They know this call will follow them

Sparse like a calling, by its own accord
Flushed at the intersection of turquoise
Birds dive into a fresh-cut horizon
Her throat swells with clouds of salt

Was this the way his ancestors lived?
Memory entombed within
Geography was never the exemption

Never in a straight line
Isis continued to wander into night
Crossing from one field to the next
Making her way to the outer edge

When the fruit of the tree falls to earth
Something is there to meet it
Darkened by the shade above
It follows its own path downward

And she began to speak
To those who stand in opposition of altruism
God gave you agency
That one day you may discover it

O son of the dance
Like a rock shadow
You must learn to split this life in two wholes
Find meaning in every sip to quench your thirst
As clouds tumble through the sky

Isis left the city square
Hoping to disappear the buildings
To her back
She walked into a new day

They told him how they'd make him new
Gave him labor half the week
Sang his praise before his face
But every smile excised his poise

There is a passion in the measured lines of her palms
As she learns to work for second chances
A revivifying melody bounces through her head
She finds the step to push on through

Illiteracy is silence
A night to bury the calligrapher's pen
A hidden chorus in the alley light

Sullen was her wait
As the world stood still
She fought herself to feel for something more
Prayed the ash of resistance into kohl
And painted her eyes to see

Maybe the world is not what it seems
Borrowing from the root for water
Suspended in its own sulcus
Trading skins for skins

When her child first arrived
She understood the contrarian view
She buried shells in the sand
Each with a name tucked inside

Tekla found his love in an open market
Fumes and fabrics tangled together
He felt an elastic vibration
Knew his steps would forever change

She could not yet see the day
Knew that something familiar stood before her
She borrowed a face from the woman next door
And descended the steps

He was made angry
By the wicked words
Of those who did not see the gathering
A bouquet of bodies standing demure
Leaning into silent change

She thumbed the rough of a bottle cap
And thought of drought
Could not shake the image of blood pooling on sand
Opened her eyes to the shimmering city

If every day he had to say again
That change will not come without struggle
If every moment someone called his bluff
He knew he'd never become one of them

                                    Isis knew this was the time
                                    Armed with a voice and body
                                    She raised her arms to the sky
                                    And swallowed her saliva

                                    How do you disappear fear?
                                    Quelled by a misremembering
                                    Shorn by time's scissors
                                    Made hot by the starry night

There is more to this
Than a friendly mask
A dictator swallows the clouds for shade
And the people are left beneath the sun
As fire rages in their spines

A breeze reminds us of redemption
The heat of bodies packed together in a steel cage
Praying only for a small bit of wind

She watched as the bodies vanished in the crowd
Capitulating to the heat as the men drag them away
The white of their shirts her last sight of them
As blood dropped slowly from their faces

The elation was too much to bear
Celebrants could only see before them
They could not see the masqueraders in the alleyway
Had no sense of the underside

She reached beneath her feet to pull a chunk of wood
Shaped like a human heart
She traced the spiral pattern that the insects bore
And closed her eyes for silence

The start of something, unlike that before
But how would they know who could lead the way?
Desperation from the weight of what was
Stunned from the prospect of now
And the journey of removal before them

In the square, the youth chant boldly
Know that anything melancholy is worthy of song
They tie their hearts together with invisible string
And strum the rhythm of destiny

From past to future, what will remain?
Weighed skillfully like the carver's tools
Hieroglyphs etched into stone, he sits silently
Like the ancient artifacts locked in colonial museums

She had always yearned for hopeful days
No matter what had become of the streets
No matter the disappearance of men in her life
No matter how small they asked her to be

At this age, change seemed absurd to some
They sat in a confusion as the streets grew to life
Amazed at the way the sun looked new

Ululate one time
She told her neighbor
Let your voice be heard in this strange new throng
Who thought the old could live to see this far?
Let our shudder rise on high

When the news reached home
The village was alive with fire
And all the children raised dust with their feet

II

The Emergence

Amid the havoc Tekla received the news
In the dusty marble hall
He was told the paperwork was complete
The time to toast their journey was near
But something in him asked forgiveness
Something in him made a space for distance

Isis began to order her thoughts
One after the other she manifested her dreams
Rubbed her hand on her belly
As she thought fondly of the palm-lined road
That led from her childhood home to school

The clouds bore heavy rain
Brazen in its pronouncement
A sign of something somewhere
Each drop an indication

The plane lifts
And from the window to the land below
Oh, how she longed to jump
Root herself to the vanishing earth

Understanding he does not walk in turbulent skies
He sinks his feet into saturated soil
The marshland wise and lofty

Tekla reminds himself, he knows no perfect men
In the path of a wake they swim
Swallow salt to remember their lungs

All things find their way, he tells himself
Like the meeting of sky and water
What becomes of a journey is read in the dust
What matters of a man is the way he walks

                                    Put to a paper test
                              Isis sold her country's soul
                                   In an effort to honor
                              And make their name anew

The heart seeks outlet
Lights a small shadow
The rippling creek always reminiscent
Like the endless guzzle of Ammit

Perhaps there is no land of parity
No understanding of a center song
What comes of this migration
May never be understood

If doubt is a buoy
The salient will rise
Break the wake of remembrance
And ratify the toil

Stranded in a sea of miasma
These newly arrived chant their way through pavement
A hope to return known earth to itself

The sound of new feet
Trailing this new dust
Over a land of ambiguity
She learns to turn her eyes from nearby shores
And swallow the mountain trail

In her dreams she's standing among the towering cane
Kneeling to place the soil between her palms
Memory by touch
A water-scented earth

He needs no proof of his humanity
Existence on a rolling dune
In the river of this cortège
He hums beneath the leaves of acacia

Taut with foreign expectation
Isis believed her way onto this land
Caught in a ruminant net

                    He learns to stand back
                    Find the line to trace
               Fold each moment into another
     He learns to block the space around his heart

Oh, great exegeses
Can a moment be defined?
We have yet to find a common road
The excursion becomes a pilgrimage
We move from border to border
Make waste of our own breath

                              Is this why we have abandoned home
                                  Set our course to the outer reach
                      Searching for a thing made of vile imagination?

The mark of erasure is carved in stone
He runs his fingers across the blank rock
With hopes to carve his own testimony

There is one reason, Tekla declares
To become anything
What you are in the great dark of winter
What you are in the great folds of summer

Isis reached inside her winter coat
Could not fathom how she'd strayed so far
The world back home was anew
And only here on this placid street could she remain

He wondered why he worked so hard
To be reconciled in a place of no elation
He could not take his countrymen by hand
And sing the songs their fathers once sung

She wondered what would come of the crescent and the cross
Could they find a new order
A way for one to never shadow the other?
She wondered if possibility was possible

"We think we are free"
"My brothers, you are!"
The line hummed like darkness across the sea
"What remains before us, is to be seen"
Silence, as the note lingered

Tekla could not fathom a nation new
Could not hold back his excitement
Held in his throat the fire of silence

Isis thought again of the palm-lined road
Wondered about the children back home
Kicking stones on the road to school
Scuffing their only good shoes

They sat together, quietly
As the baby cooed herself to sleep
They could not find their place
No longer here or there

Isis knew that Tekla could not bear the distance
They told themselves what was best for the family
Absolved their guilt by claiming safety
Dreamt each night of throwing rocks

III

The Migration

To settle from one geography to another
Seemed to make no difference
Tekla was strange in a strange land
Chance was the culture he yearned
To resettle once and again was now a matter of taste
Nothing could be bound, it seemed
Everything tethered would soon vanish

Isis watched as the imprints on the footpath increased
Held by a small reflection of light
She caught her thoughts in midair
Broken only by her child's laughter
She wondered what she might remember
In a place where all she did was learn

When he woke that winter morning
He understood that heat could overcome cold
He walked the streets transfigured
Imagined the multiplicity of his face

The news came quick
Like a memory escaped from a dark hollow
The dead were mounting in number
Each a similar name

How swiftly they turned from present to past
Could not find a name for prudence
Rested on a broken crutch

Solidarity?
What choice have we now?
Justice is the one staff for freedom's flag
How can we share with the enemy our voice?
Violence comes from the mind's core

If unshackling were a song
I'd slide my palm on skin
And watch it trail to air

Forgive my days of fullness, he prayed
In this land of filch, let my wares be witness
Sokar, bless these hands with flourish
As my heart is weighed against a feather

The bones of possibility, laid to rest
Stratum, the root's architecture
Isis' map floats in an ocean sweep
And what can we exhume from this great distance?

Every time he looks to this sea
He is reminded of his own humanity
With every shuffled step
He recalls everything that is left

Intrinsic is her name
Isis' calling buried dead
Antiquity, enigmatic wonder
History a chafe of surface and burn
Cracked light into woven earth

Who desiccated the darkness
In the nation of wont?
Shading their day from the pelagic road
Stripped the bark of verdure from the day

Their bodies have absorbed this poison
Flanked by an iridescence
Fraught by the way of home

If cartography were a bird
Would she dot her notes on a river bottom?
Would she croon her maps on a mountain ridge?
Would her cadence lead us home?

Tekla tells a story of come and gone
Carves the mask of dignity
Makes a place for fire

Nefer is the land
Stolen in her grace
Made part by the legacy of hunger
The flock of wingless birds

What if we were free
Like the facilities of Africa
The taking of an anomaly
The mapping of rout
Assembled at the edge of the desert

Harmony makes a road
To the victim's haven
We must not tell of wisdom's knots

He seeks refuge in the shade of acacia
Stolen on the land of sand
Loose is the root in decadence

From this canopy of thirst
Release comes
This is sovereignty
This is the story of hope

Like the order of a midnight office
Begin believing
Say loudly everything that need be said
Train your feet to walk the night

If every wanderer touched the sky
Was made full by Sah's direction
Spoken in another language
Premonition would be their freedom

In the hail of lead
We were made to understand our veins
Forget the vestiture of desire
Cloak ourselves in an impeding life

From the sinister gaze of the Atlantic
Its mouth curling with foam
Swept between a desolation
Isis found her way

Every memory
Became a home of its own
Despite the illusion
A reminder that nothing stagnant could be held

This skin he remembered
Borrowed from the hide of his kin
Tekla carried on this wanting

IV

The Settling

This was their sanctuary now
Tomorrow was never a promise
Tekla worked for his longing
And stole glances at his own recollection
Felt himself on a floating expanse
Balanced between land and air

Isis knew that as her child grew
Her past would become an obscurity
A story told by a distant teller
She knew now the way that snow could make a place new
The way history could bury itself

They sat beside one another
Smiled at the thoughts of arrival
Told the story of themselves

Anticipation a new land
Vast like an upward spire
The pain in her belly, a new inertia
And the yearning to forget

When you first arrive
Your essence, stolen
The past locked in memory
It is as if no other seed had been planted

If splendid were a tale you tell
You'd praise the past as if it hadn't pierced
You'd gather your new neighbors
And perjure all the night

And all who came before you
Lackluster in their eyes
Falter in their step

And you rise this way
Greet the morning haze
Blinded by a waning recollection
Frightened by the possibilities
Of distance being your home

How they lived too well
Replete with sorrow
They fill the jugs of empty
Drive the memory from their crowns

He wondered how tanks could rule a people
How men trained for killing can make a nation
How a nation can make men for killing

She watched from afar as her sister bled
How the color of her undergarment shaped the landscape
The sinister tread of black boots made for flesh
One calloused hand forcing another

If he were there now
Would he stand and chant the dusk to light
Would he stay the night by his child's side
Strum the oud for reverie
If he were there now?

                                        In one place
                        Isis felt a stranger due to ritual
                                    In another place
                        She felt stranger due to birth

Tekla declared his love
In the frigid wind
No longer did he speak of a nation
His love was for a land and a people
How he yearned for a return

None among her understood her nerves
They could not know release, having never felt a snare
Maybe it was a semblance of reality
A resonance of another humanity

He believed that zero was the standard
If only they could forecast a new desert
Redefine the marshland's edge
Make sovereignty from silt and sand

She asked herself if return was destined
If she could leave this toil for another
If her child could find aim in havoc
She knew her belly spoke with certainty

After years of building something new
Conviction vanished
Anywhere was here
Definition a fabrication in the story

What can we call home?
Will the heart suffice?
Is scent enough to make our lives feel whole?
Shall I keep the pot to cook ceaselessly?
How does the soil make us firm?

                              The square is our false door
                    Our chants, a prayer for all who disappeared
                    We must not be mired in the present and forget

                    To acknowledge victory, one must not succumb
                    If every thread we knot is untangled by dread
                        We can only learn to weave once more
                          Stain our fingers with new dye

The youth are bold with tenacity
Recumbent only to dream
They make a vow to trust
And laughter to overshadow sway

Counting on her slender fingers
The number who have called her names
Have taken claim to what cannot be owned
Her voice a strident anthem

We will know to be
Unified by vigor
None of us shall be left by the wayside
No place for women is no place for men
This struggle, or no struggle

Let the people decide
Let the sphinx be our witness
Let the day be new like the Song of Solomon
That our hearts may abide

In every elevated hand, the lines for tomorrow
Pleading with open palms
That their life can match their spirit
That their stretch might reach the sky

The sin is to come with your own
To march the streets with a predetermined strut
To shape the rock before you know its quarry
Only a bird can trace the sky

If we can make this plight our daily
Can fill the gulf with laughter
Our meditation could make for a nation

How long can we hold?
Power must succumb
To irrigate, we need the water wheel
Abundant our crops, bountiful our glory
Vital is this life we make

There is a difficulty on these mild streets
To roam in a place without an antecedent
Untethered, an illusion of freedom

Memory its own remembering
She made nostalgia of an arduous life
Knowing her longing was emblematic
She struggled with the argot

Do we travel so far only for an enclave?
Tekla could not see the way they saw
Could not make himself at home
Would never understand the distances of heart

No matter how many generations are born to this soil
There will always be a sense of hunger
A yearning to swim in an open sea
An empyrean calling

I have made my peace
He says to himself
I have found the note that makes my voice call
I have swallowed emptiness, to be full
I have seen color everywhere

What this life can become
Is what this life will be worth
There will be no standard in the spine of a man
No guide in the face of a woman

A man must shout from the hollow of his body
A man must learn to stretch in an open field
A man must learn to strum his wish
A man must learn simply to speak

Oh, how I feel alright!
She takes the sun from on high
Calls it by its old name
Culls the strength of her own ribs

If I can learn to make a place
I will bellow from the balls of my feet
Brush each child's hair for strength

I'm to put it on
Wear each joy like stone
Lord, the coming is in the returning
We will take to the skies with our own wings
Wherever we land is home

Give me this strength
No man shall make me his own
I call upon each descendant

The foolish zealots have forgotten
Could not find the road that leads to a fork
Cannot make a way from solemn ties
They've been cursed by the god of inundation

He could not fathom what has become
Where was the magnitude of his youth?
And who were these men of foreign promise?
These songless spirits cursing his land

Oh how she burned for exuberance
To learn to dance in her children's feet
To blanket the square with linen
And watch the people drift

He will chant a psalm
Give thanks, oh Most High
Why should I masquerade and bury my roots?
It's no matter if men don't like my faith
My voice is my only spear

Isis could not help but smile
The way the young could carry on
The way their cynicism could make the sun rise
Theirs was a glorious resolution

Remarkable in their narrowness
Why must a nation share one symbol?
Like the papyrus of the north and the lotus of the south
Plurality has its place

If this could make a life feel fresh
She was willing to stumble
To make fire from the ashes of disaster
To become a falcon, paddling the air

Never would regret cross his brow
Aspiration was a shell to the ear
A rising tide salt-full of hope

She heard the echo
Imminent return
One could not sort this land from the other
Something in each became their only freedom
Their lives now bifurcated

Sediment in the delta of diaspora
Made from the mouths of their kin
Their stories would forever cross seas

When the ocean casts its light
Hers was a roving mind
No longer a caltrop in her path
She learned to sing with variance

He remembered the way his father used to speak
Assured of a trajectory that led to this moment
Unquestioning of intercession
Trusting in the hands of others

She watched the bougainvillea climb
Ornament of her youth, coloring memory
How one plant could survive in divergent places
She plucked it for her hair and wore it as an emblem

I'll take the same path
I'll plant the same trees
I'll learn to live in visibility
I'll honor the bones and ask them for guidance
I'll make familiar this habit

Make my offenses a quiet yearning
Turn my thoughtless heart to succor
Make my hands a respite of hope
And let me call nowhere my home

How can a man call his home a nation
If his own heart is disunited
If he wanders from his children's wants
Cannot hear the open notes of their thirst?

Memory is the residence of truth
Sheltering scars from the wind
She shapes the clay with her fingertips
Places each thought in the lip of a bowl

His heart had learned to saunter
Move between the borders of its cavity
Finding the liminal brush
Sprouting from the red earth
Each step a register of earth and sky

My children will learn to call
They will learn the words for freedom
They will learn to walk with splintered feet

She dreamt of the square
Children in her arms
Feet rooted to the pavement of her past
She watched as all their memories transformed
Hummed a song of remembrance

ACKNOWLEDGMENTS

Special thanks to the editors of the following journals where sections of this poem previously appeared: *Eleven Eleven,* California College of the Arts; *Platte Valley Review,* University of Nebraska, Kearney; and *MELUS: Multi-Ethnic Literature of the United States.*

Eternal respect to: Chris Abani for his agility, laughter, and consistent chant; Antwi Akom for his visionary spirit and solo riffs; Kwame Dawes for his stalwart presence and rock steady; and John Carlos Perea for the never-ending bass line. And a debt of gratitude to my editor, Parneshia Jones, and all the staff at Northwestern University Press.

Tahrir The word means "liberation" in Arabic and is also a reference to Tahrir Square in downtown Cairo. On February 11, 2011, after eighteen days of protest in Tahrir Square, the Egyptian people overthrew President Hosni Mubarak, who had ruled Egypt for thirty years. On June 30, 2013, a second wave of protests began, which swelled into a revolution directed at toppling elected president Mohamed Morsi. On July 3, 2013, President Morsi was overthrown, and the Egyptian military took control of the government. The weeks and months ensuing became some of the bloodiest and most divisive in modern Egyptian history.

Ammit A frightening creature who lives near the scales of justice. Ancient Egyptians believed that, at death, a person's heart is weighed on the scales of justice. If the heart fails the test, the person is not granted eternal life, and Ammit devours the heart.

Sokar An ancient Egyptian god of the necropolis in Memphis, Sokar is often shown with a human body and the head of a hawk. Although his origins are obscure, he is believed to have been a patron of craftsmen as well as a god of fertility.

Nefer In ancient Egyptian, the hieroglyphic sign most often depicted to mean "goodness" or "beauty."

Sah The ancient Egyptian god who presided over the constellation commonly called Orion.

False door A common architectural element on tombs in ancient Egypt, the false door was a place where one could leave gifts and prayers asking for the intervention of the deceased.